Contents

The ideas and material in this booklet were developed during the course of the Exeter Extending Literacy (EXEL) Project, which was funded by the Nuffield Foundation

Published by the Reading and Language Information Centre, 1997
The University of Reading
Bulmershe Court
Earley
Reading RG6 1HY

Designed and produced by Text Matters

Introduction

In spite of the controversies and debates of the past few years, the evidence suggests that most teachers do a good job of teaching children to read. Yet the evidence also tells us there are important gaps. It seems that teachers have always had some difficulty in teaching children to read information, or non-fiction, texts.

Practical ways to teach reading for information is based on the experience of the Exeter Extending Literacy (EXEL) Project. It outlines a series of teaching strategies which teachers might use to help children become more proficient in this crucial area. It offers suggestions about:

- **The nature of reading for information and finding out**
  Why do children find this activity difficult and why do they so often resort to copying?

- **The use of previous knowledge and the setting of questions**
  How can children be encouraged to draw on their existing knowledge and ask questions to guide their information searching?

- **The location of information**
  How can information retrieval skills be taught in meaningful ways?

- **Making sense of information on the page**
  How can teachers enhance children's interactions with texts?

- **Critical reading**
  What does it mean to read critically and how can teachers encourage this approach?

- **Integrating reading for information into classroom practice**
  How can teachers build this kind of work into class topics?

Finding out

Zoe is a ten-year-old with learning difficulties. Her class is studying 'Living things' as their topic and, for this lesson, Zoe and her group have been asked to choose a particular living thing which interests them and to 'find out about it'. Zoe and her friends have chosen dolphins and have picked out several information books from their class collection. For the next 45 minutes or so they work quietly and diligently.

Towards the end of the lesson Zoe's support teacher arrives and goes across to check on what the girls have done. She sees the piece of writing shown in figure 1 and asks Zoe to read out what she has written. Zoe finds this nearly impossible to do. The teacher also asks what Zoe thinks she has learnt about dolphins, but she has very few ideas.

figure 1 Zoe's writing

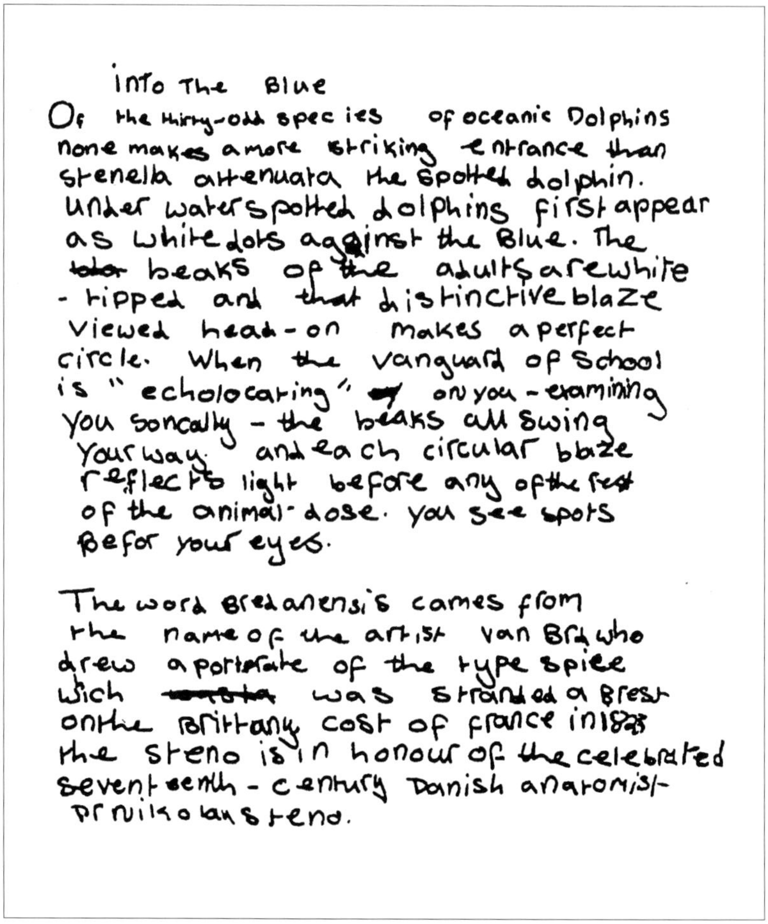
Into The Blue
Of the thirty-odd spec ies of oceanic Dolphins
none makes a more striking entrance than
stenella attenuata the spotted dolphin.
Under water spotted dolphins first appear
as white dots against the Blue. The
beaks of the adults are white
- tipped and that distinctive blaze
viewed head-on makes a perfect
circle. When the vanguard of school
is "echolocating" on you - examining
you soncally - the beaks all swing
your way. and each circular blaze
reflects light before any of the rest
of the animal-dose. you see spots
befor your eyes.

The word bredanensis comes from
the name of the artist van Bred who
drew a portorate of the type spiee
wich was stranded a Brest
on the Brittany cost of france in 1828
the steno is in honour of the celebrated
seventeenth-century Danish anatomist
Dr Niklolans steno.

Most primary teachers will recognise what has happened here. Zoe has copied, word for word, from one or more information books. She has not processed what she has written beyond simply recognising that it is about dolphins. She has learnt very little from the lesson.

The research of the EXEL project suggests that most primary children know that they should not copy directly from information books. Many can give good reasons for this. Eight-year-old Anna, for example, told us that 'you learn a lot more if you write it in your own words'. Yet, faced with finding out from books, most children at some stage resort to copying. Why is this so common and how can teachers help children read for information more effectively?

The task and the text

An important part of the problem seems to be the nature of the task. Zoe has been asked to 'find out about' a topic but needs help to narrow the focus. As she discovers, there are whole books on dolphins. How can she choose among all this information? In order to make the task more manageable, she needs help to decide what she wants to find out before looking at the books.

Even if children manage to use 'information retrieval skills' to locate material on the required topic, they often experience difficulties with the text. Children in primary classrooms tend to lack experience of the different genres of non-fiction and their organisational structures. They find the linguistic features – vocabulary, connectives, cohesion, register – associated with non-fiction more difficult than those in more familiar narrative texts. A number of teaching strategies provide support and make the activity of reading information much more purposeful.

What do I know and what do I want to know?

The support teacher decided to introduce a different approach to the task and at the end of the lesson Zoe had produced a very different piece of writing about dolphins (see figure 2).

How had the support teacher moved Zoe on from passive copying to undertaking her own research?

3

figure 2 Zoe's second piece of writing

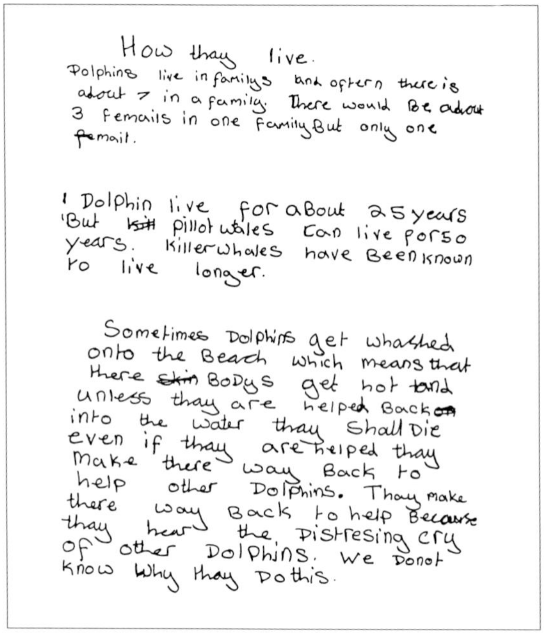

How thay live.
Dolphins live in familys and oftern there is about 7 in a family. There would Be about 3 femails in one Family But only one femail.

I Dolphin live for aBout 25 years But pillot wales can live porso years. Killerwhales have Been known to live longer.

Sometimes Dolphins get whashed onto the Beach which means that there BoDys get hot and unless thay are helped Back into the water thay Shall Die even if thay are helped thay make there way Back to help other Dolphins. Thay make there way Back to help Because thay hear the, Distresing cry of other Dolphins. We Donot know why thay Do this.

The first step was to close all of the information books Zoe had been using. Zoe was then asked two of the most crucial questions in the process of reading for information:

- What do I know already about this topic?
- What do I want to know about it?

Why are these questions so important? A great deal of research points to the importance of children's previous knowledge in their understanding of new knowledge (Anderson & Pearson, 1984; Anderson, 1977). It is also important that this previous knowledge is brought to the forefront of the learner's mind, that is, made explicit, if it is to be useful (Bransford, 1983).

Another approach that we have found specially useful is the KWL grid, consisting of three columns: What I **K**now? What I **W**ant to know? What did I **L**earn? This is a simple but effective strategy which takes children through the different steps of the research process at the same time as recording their learning.

The support teacher introduced Zoe to the strategy by drawing a KWL as three columns in her jotter. She then asked Zoe what she already knew about dolphins and scribed her responses under the first heading (see figure 3a). In the early stages, teacher modelling is very important. Only when children are thoroughly familiar with the strategy should they be asked to attempt the task independently.

figure 3a Part of Zoe's KWL

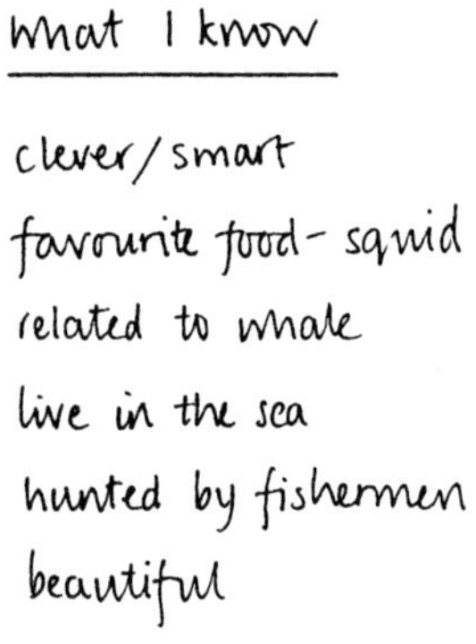

What I know

clever/smart
favourite food- squid
related to whale
live in the sea
hunted by fishermen
beautiful

figure 3b Part of Zoe's KWL

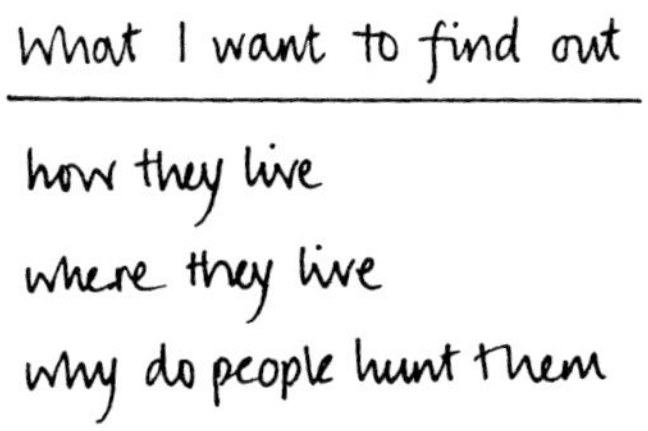

What I want to find out
_____

how they live

where they live

why do people hunt them

Not only did this tapping into previous knowledge have a vital role to play in helping Zoe understand the texts, but it also gave her an active role in the topic right from the beginning.

The next stage was to help her establish a purpose for her reading by asking what she wanted to know now. The usual formulation of the task, as in 'find out about', is far too broad to be useful: it is unclear whether children are required to fill a postcard or a book. Discussing and recording what she already knew allowed Zoe to generate further questions which interested her. Again, these were scribed by the teacher (see figure 3b).

On this occasion, Zoe and her teacher decided to concentrate on just one question (they only had an hour together) and she was encouraged to brainstorm around 'How do they live?' Again her teacher scribed and the resultant concept map can be seen in Figure 4.

figure 4 Zoe's concept map

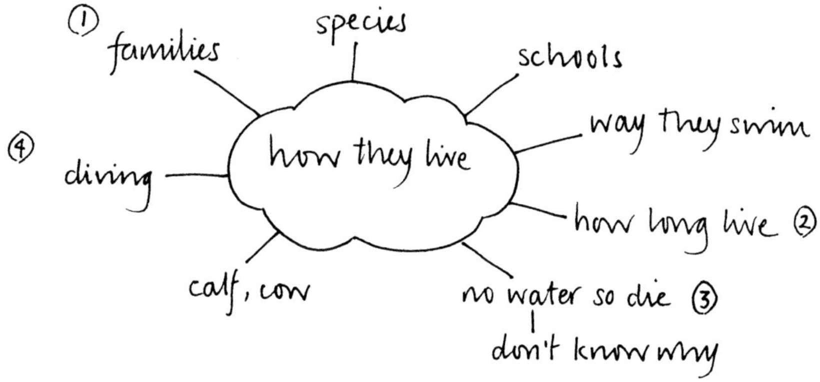

① families   species   schools   way they swim
④ diving — *how they live* — how long live ②
calf, cow   no water so die ③
don't know why

Additional questions under the heading 'How do they live?' were numbered to keep the process clear and manageable and, at this point, Zoe was ready to return to her information books to find the answers. Now she also had key words which she could use to search the index and contents. Sometimes her teacher wrote the word on a piece of card so that she could run it down the index or the page and match the word. This gave her practice in scanning. We can see from the writing she had completed by the end of the session (figure 2) that she was working her way logically through the questions (she had tackled 1 and 2). Not only had she learnt something about dolphins but this had also been a powerful lesson on how to do research.

Extending the approach

Grids such as the KWL not only provide a written record of children's approaches to reading for information; the format also acts as an organiser, helping children see more clearly the stages of research. This approach offers a logical structure for tackling research tasks in many areas of the curriculum.

Of course, when children are asked what they know about something, there is no guarantee that what they say will in fact be accurate. For instance, two Year 3 girls recorded 'They live in straw houses' among the facts they already knew about the Vikings. This was then used as a focus for the children's own research, allowing them to play an active role in correcting their misconception.

The grid can also be extended by the addition of a fourth column: KWFL – where the F stands for 'Where will I **F**ind the information?' An example of this can be seen in Figure 5 which records the research of a Year 5 class into Kenya.

figure 5 A completed KWFL grid

Kenya

What do I KNOW?

1. Kenya is a very poor country.
2. Lots of crops grow in kenya.
3. They have a church
4. They carry jugs and bowls of water on their heads.
5. It is a very hot country.
6. Everybody is black.
7. They have animals to help them grow their crops.
8. Some people live in huts.

What do I WANT to know?

1. How many people live in kenya?
2. What sort of names do you have.
3. What is your main meal that you eat?
4. What sort of jobs do you have?
5. Why do women do all the hard work?
6. How many t.v sets do you have.
7. What age do people leave school.

Where will I FIND the information

1. In the school library.
2. Write to the kenya Tourist information Centre.
3. Look in an atlas.
4. Ask Mrs Dingle.
5. Ask Lisa's uncle.
6. Look in a geography magazine.
7. In Books.
8. Leaflets.

What have I LEARNT?

1. Kenya has 21000000 people living there They have names like
2. Rosia, Godfrey, Julia,
3. Maize, yams and cassava (tropical plant like a potato)
4. Ploughing, growing crops, making huts, collecting wood for the fire.
6. Kenya has over 200,000 TV sets.

The grid shows that the children realise that there are sources of useful information in addition to books. (Mrs Dingle, of course, is the fount of wisdom in the classroom who might be expected to know everything there was to know!)

Another useful grid is the QUADS grid which consists of 4 columns: Questions, Answer, Details, Source. This, too, provides a simple framework for recording information, including the child's questions. Figure 6 shows the QUADS grid of a seven-year-old researching the diplodocus. The class had initially shared all they knew about dinosaurs before each child selected one to feature in their own story.

figure 6 A QUADS grid about the diplodocus

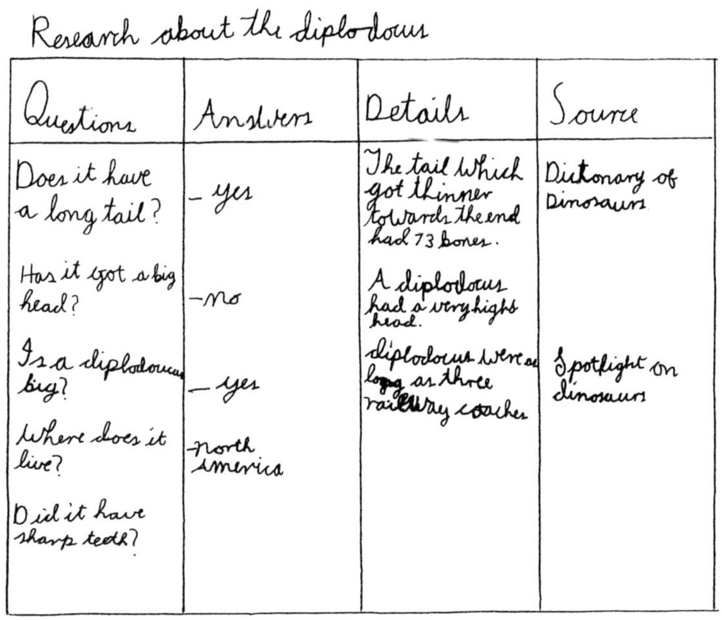

Research about the diplodocus

Questions	Answers	Details	Source
Does it have a long tail?	— yes	The tail which got thinner towards the end had 73 bones.	Dictonary of Dinosaurs
Has it got a big head?	—no	A diplodocus had a very light head.	
Is a diplodocus big?	— yes	diplodocus were as long as three railway coaches	Spotlight on dinosaurs
Where does it live?	north america		
Did it have sharp teeth?			

An interesting feature of the QUADS grid is the splitting of the answer into answer/details. Children are required to summarise first and then give details, a notion which can be discussed in terms of the 'short' answer and the 'long' answer. This approach can be very useful in moving children away from mere copying.

The inclusion of the Source column fosters another useful study skill. Children are asked to note where they found the information in case they need to check or share it with another. Seven-year-old Lee is using this grid for the first time and has not recorded his source fully. He may find it useful to note details such as page numbers and authors. With support from his teacher, he will undoubtedly refine the skill.

Finding the answers

Locating information involves children first in making decisions about where they might find the required information and then in using specific study skills, such as using an index or searching a data base. The problems lie not with the skills themselves, but in children's readiness to select and use the appropriate strategy. They may know how to use an index, consult a library catalogue, use a CD-ROM but, when engaged on an information finding task, often fail to use such strategies. Instead they may browse through a book, randomly search a shelf of books, ask a friend and so on. We would go further and argue that the mismatch between what pupils 'know' in their heads and what they actually do when confronted with a real task may well be related to how these skills are taught.

Exercises or worksheets are often devised to teach 'study skills'. Children are given an index, for example, and then asked questions which require them to use it. After completing several worksheets of this kind, it is assumed that they will be able to use index pages. Most teachers will, however, have experience which contradicts this claim. We need to teach information finding in more contextualised ways.

Using non-fiction 'big books'

Many publishers now offer big versions of non-fiction books aimed at both key stage 1 and key stage 2 audiences. These allow teachers to model to groups of children appropriate information finding strategies, skim reading, scanning for a specific item and so on. The teacher can demonstrate what you need to do by giving a running commentary. For example, a group of children had asked 'How long does a chick stay a chick?' Using the big book version of *The life of a duck* (Magic Beans series, Heinemann, 1989), the teacher modelled how they might use an information book to answer their question. As she did so, she talked about what she was doing and why. She thus made what is usually an internal monologue accessible to the children. The conversation went something like:

'Now, Joanne asked about chicks growing into ducks. How can I see if this book has anything on chicks? What shall do I do? Shall I read it from the beginning? No that would take too long? I could look in the index. This list of words at the back that tells me what's in the book. Yes, I can look in the index. Let's look up chicks in the index. So I'm going to turn to the back of the book. Here it is. Index. Now. Its arranged alphabetically a… b… so c should be next … here it is. C. Can anybody see the word chick in this column?' And so on…

This kind of modelling gives the children some very important lessons on what an experienced reader does. The teacher's vocalisation provides a 'learning script' which children can 'parrot' for themselves. Younger and/or inexperienced learners will often talk themselves through a task but, as they become more skilled, the script becomes internalised. Finally, it operates almost unconsciously, only called to the surface again in tricky situations.

Interacting with information text

A variety of strategies help children engage more productively with the text. The two we have found to be of major benefit are text marking and text restructuring.

Text marking

Text marking techniques such as underlining are used by many adults when they wish to note something in a text as being of significance. Of course, we cannot encourage children to write on school books, but they can use text marking on teacher-prepared information sheets or on photocopies of pages from books. We need to use the strategy in a focused way, for example, by using different colours to mark information in response to particular questions.

Children might also be asked to underline the sentence they think contains the main idea of a text. Different children may choose to underline different sentences and this can be used as a discussion point when they share and justify their decisions. They can also be asked to underline the most important sentence in each paragraph. Putting these sentences together should give them an outline summary of the whole passage.

Text can also be numbered to identify sequences of events. This is especially useful where steps in a process are separated by chunks of text and there is a danger of losing the thread.

Text restructuring

The essence of this strategy is to encourage children to read and then present the information in some other way. In doing so they have to 'pass the information through their brain' – that is, work at understanding it. Restructuring also gives teachers access to children's levels of understanding and can be a useful assessment strategy.

There are many different ways of text restructuring. Figure 7 shows the work from Year 5 children after reading a text on mummification in Ancient Egypt. They marked the text to show the stages of the process and then drew a series of pictures to represent these stages. The next day, and without further access to the original text, they wrote captions to accompany their pictures.

figure 7 Text restructuring: mummification

1. When someone had died they took out liver, stomach and intestines. Then they put them in Canopic jars.

2. Then they took the brain out through the nostrils.

3. They washed the body in oils and perfumes before covering with naphtha.

4. After that they wrapped the body in long bandages.

5. Good luck charms were put all over the body.

6. The mummy was then put in a coffin and buried in a tomb.

Text restructuring can be used with quite young children. Five-year-old Kim, for example, having been read the big book *The life of a duck* by her teacher, showed the life cycle of a duck by means of a diagram (figure 8a).

Her teacher was very pleased but then asked Kim to find how long the process took. Kim consulted the book for herself and then added to her diagram (Figure 8b).

figures 8a & 8b
Text restructuring: the life of a duck, parts 1 & 2

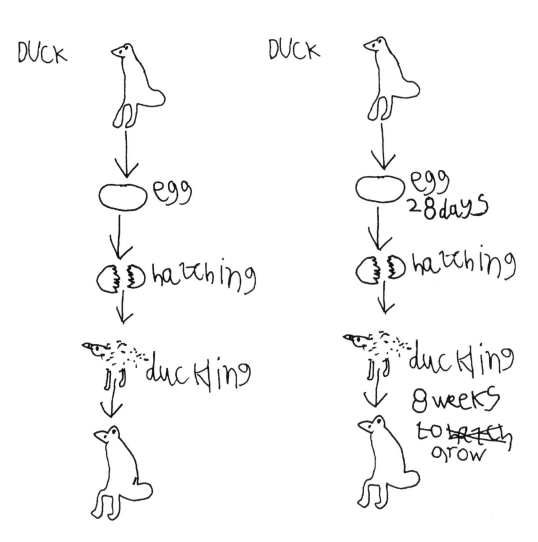

Genre exchange

Restructuring can also take place by asking children to transpose something from one written genre into another. A group of ten-year-olds, for example, had read about scribes in Ancient Egypt. They might simply have been asked to write about what they had read 'in their own words' and this would most likely have led to a good deal of copying from the original. This time, however, they were asked to rewrite the information they had gathered in the form of a job advertisement (figure 9).

figure 9 Genre exchange: scribes

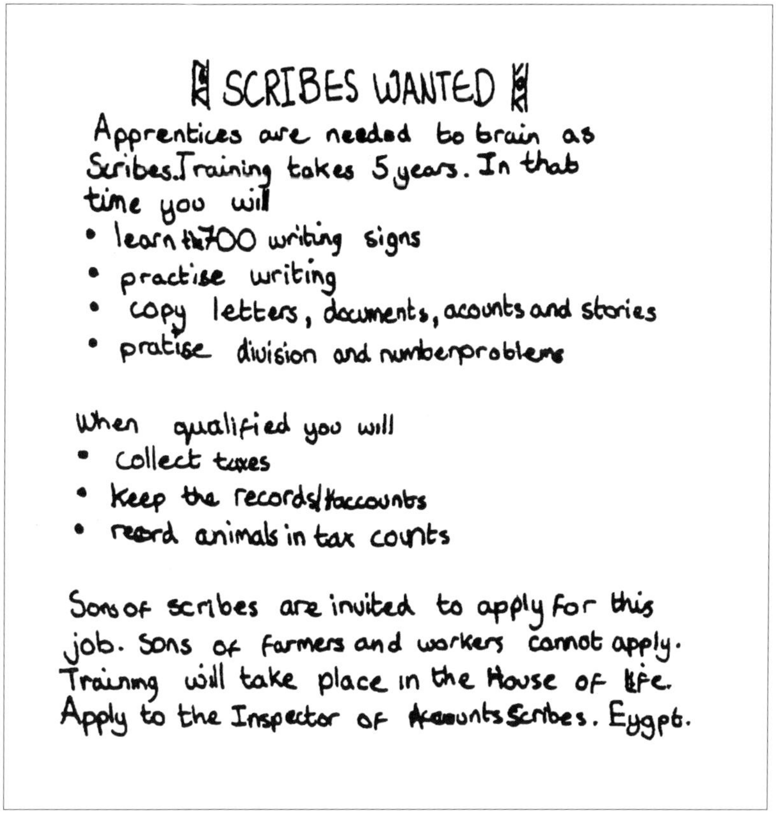
SCRIBES WANTED

Apprentices are needed to train as Scribes. Training takes 5 years. In that time you will

- learn 700 writing signs
- practise writing
- copy letters, documents, acounts and stories
- pratise division and numberproblems

When qualified you will

- collect taxes
- keep the records/accounts
- record animals in tax counts

Sons of scribes are invited to apply for this job. Sons of farmers and workers cannot apply. Training will take place in the House of Life. Apply to the Inspector of Accounts Scribes. Eygpt.

This 'playing' with genres not only forces children to reorganise their material – itself an aid to comprehension – but also gives vital experience of a variety of genres and guides them away from simple copying.

Critical reading

Most people would agree that, when we teach children to read for information, we also need to teach them to be critical about what they read. Several approaches help children become more aware of bias and propaganda.

Encourage active discussion of texts

Discussion should not only centre on what texts mean. Other questions might include:

- Who produced this text?
  - What are their qualifications for doing so?
- What is its purpose?
- What choices were made during its production?
  - What formats, structures, vocabulary were rejected?
  - Why were these choices made?
  - What if different choices had been made?

Such questions might seem difficult, but there is evidence that even quite young children are capable of discussing them if the context is right. Jennifer O'Brien (1994), for example, describes how she asked the following question to a class of six-year-olds after reading *The fantastic Mr Fox:* 'In this story, Roald Dahl shows Mrs Fox to be weak and scared. Draw a different Mrs Fox helping to save her family. Use speech bubbles and labels to show what she could say and do to save her family.' The children drew pictures of a strong and adventurous Mrs Fox planning and digging to save her family. New versions of texts where different choices are made offer many exciting possibilities.

Children can also examine different versions of the same story and talk about why changes have been made. They might, for example, compare Jon Scieska's *The true story of the three little pigs* with traditional version(s). There are plenty of examples of such 'fractured fairy tales' to choose from.

Confront children with texts which arise from different viewpoints

This often happens quite naturally. One group of nine-year-olds, for example, came across a dispute in the books they were reading while working on a project on 'Space'. One book claimed that Saturn had 15 moons, another that it had 16 moons. At first the children simply wanted to know which of these books was telling the truth and which was 'lying'. In fact, the situation was more complex. When the dates of publication were examined, it was found that there was a ten year gap between the books. The teacher and the children reasoned, therefore, that in this period scientists had probably discovered a new moon around Saturn.

The fact that information does not remain static is an important realisation for children which can be encouraged by contrasting older and newer books on a similar subject. Compare, for example, books about computers published more than about fifteen years ago with the latest volumes. In one source, computers fill rooms and store data on large, whirling tapes: in another they fit on desks and in pockets and store data on small square 'discs' or objects like credit cards.

There are, of course, many sources of discrepancy. A class of eight year olds studying the Norman invasion of Britain in 1066 was fascinated to find that accounts by Norman and Anglo-Saxon chroniclers told radically different stories. Their teacher's response to the inevitable question, 'Who's telling the truth?' was to explain that, in all probability, nobody was. The nature of historical records is such that it is almost impossible for there not to be a 'point of view' in the writing. As any Black South African, native American, or Scot will testify, what counts as history is almost always told from the point of view of the victors.

Children can be introduced to this idea by studying contrasting texts. Reports of the same events from different newspapers offer an easy way in. The approach of a newspaper such as *The Daily Telegraph* is very different from *The Guardian,* and different again from *The Sun.* Children can learn a great deal by comparing the points of information, the language, pictures and headlines for the same story.

Encourage children to produce their own texts for a range of socially important purposes

Engaging in authentic activities is essential for children's learning. Purposes which are real to children tend to come from their own social world which includes school. Examples range from letters to the local council about the litter in the streets around the school to writing to persuade the headteacher that snacks should be allowed in the school playground.

Give children access to the socially agreed forms used in texts written for different purposes

Particular writing forms and structures have emerged to meet particular communication purposes. One way to make these forms explicit is to structure children's non-fiction writing through writing frames (see Lewis & Wray, 1996, for details of this approach).

The research process in action

As part of their topic on 'Change', Ms M's Year 4 class was studying how the town where they lived had changed over time. She wanted the children to use contemporary documents as well as more usual information sources, such as books, for their research.

Like most teachers, Ms M was concerned that her pupils should develop good research habits, but she wanted them to learn 'study skills' in the context of real information handling, rather than in isolated skills lessons. There was, of course, the usual range of ability and levels of literacy competence within the class. Although she was convinced that everyone should undertake what HMI describe as 'the threefold process of formulating appropriate questions, selecting and reading texts to find information and writing it up in their own words' (DES, 1989), she was worried that some of the children might find this difficult.

Ms M was interested to see how the ideas and strategies suggested by the EXEL project might work in her classroom. The term's work was guided by the EXIT model (shown on the left) developed as part of the project

EXIT: Extending interactions with text

- Activation of previous knowledge
- Establishing purposes
- Locating information
- Adopting an appropriate strategy
- Interacting with text
- Monitoring understanding
- Making a record
- Evaluating information
- Assisting memory
- Communicating information

Planning the topic

At the outset, Ms M had gathered a collection of books linked to the topic together with photographs, maps, local shop advertisements from various eras, a variety of historical sources and some artefacts. She intended to take the class on a walk along the High Street and to the parish church. Although she had planned the main historical events she wished to cover (the Great Fire of Crediton, the Civil War, changes in the High Street, changes in shopping habits, etc.), Ms M wanted the children themselves to be involved in the more detailed question setting.

The first session began by focusing on the children's prior knowledge of the Great Fire of Crediton. Schema theory (Anderson & Pearson, 1984; Wilson & Anderson, 1986) shows us that the activation of prior knowledge plays a vital role in helping children understand texts, and in making the learning of new information more effective. Foregrounding children's prior knowledge also gives them an active role in learning right from the beginning. By asking what they know, self-esteem and a sense of 'ownership' of knowledge are enhanced.

'I don't know anything'

Sometimes prior knowledge is readily accessible (for example, most children will come up with something on 'Space' or 'Families' or other such topics) and it is possible to go straight into brainstorming, concept mapping, KWL grids, etc. However, when Ms M asked the class what they knew about the Great Fire of Crediton their answers were: 'Nothing', 'I don't know anything', 'Never heard of it.'

This kind of response often occurs when children are asked direct questions on topics remote from their immediate experience, such as the Aztecs or the Ancient Greeks. The problem is not that children know nothing, but that they do not recognise which aspects of their own experience may be relevant. They need help to 'key into' what they know.

In this case the teacher probed their knowledge with a series of questions:

- 'What can you work out from the fact that it was called the Great Fire of Crediton? What does the word 'great' tell you?' (Asking the children to deduce from existing knowledge.) 'It was big... It was in Crediton.'

- 'What happens when you get a big fire?' 'People try to put it out... There is damage... Buildings get destroyed... Sometimes people get killed.' (These replies show the children drawing on their existing generic knowledge of fires.)

As the discussion progressed, several children remembered that they had heard of the Great Fire of Crediton before. This episode clearly illustrates that our memories often need jogging and talking with others is an important trigger.

As the teacher scribed the responses on the blackboard, one child volunteered that it started in a baker's shop. This was incorrect (the child was probably confusing it with the Great Fire of London). Here we see another important aspect of activating prior knowledge. Not only did the teacher have access to what the children knew, and the gaps in their knowledge, but, importantly, she also had access to their misconceptions. In this instance, Ms M. scribed the child's comment but made a mental note that, if no-one else suggested it, she would add 'Where and how the fire started?' to the research questions. Misconceptions corrected by the teacher often fail to have much impact upon children who are far more likely to change their minds if they play an active part in correcting mistakes.

Other strategies can be used when children feel they 'know nothing', but let us stay for now with Ms M. After listing the children's responses, she read them back, thus reviewing what they knew. She then asked them if there was anything they wanted to know about the fire. Questions came quickly: When was it? How did it start? Were people killed? Again the teacher scribed the questions and, at this point, was able to put a question mark after 'It started in a baker's shop'. Turning statements, whether correct or incorrect, into questions is a useful strategy.

When Ms M asked the children how and where they thought they might find the answers to their questions they came up with a range of suggestions: books, newspapers, interviews with people who were there, photographs and television reports. This was a good list for a contemporary event but it was pointed out that, as the fire had happened a long time ago, not all these sources would apply. They went through the list, reassessing the sources. As it was a local event, the children also discussed why they might find it unproductive to look in the general history books available in the classroom.

Ms M produced ten historical sources including eyewitness accounts, newspaper reports, insurance company accounts and disaster fund appeals. She explained what each was but did not read them to the children. They were then told that they were each going to decide which question(s) to research and that their final piece of work would be displayed, along with the sources, on the wall in the corridor. They were each given a QUADS sheet (see page 7) to record their work and in pairs or small groups were given a photocopied set of sources to share.

Interacting with the text

Having decided on, and written down, their questions, the children turned to the sources. There was a certain amount of initial browsing and children shared comments and puzzlement (the shape of the 's', for example, looked more like an 'f' to their modern eyes). It was not possible to use contents or index pages with these documents, but the children

were encouraged to skim over the materials looking for key words or phrases (eg fire, started, died) contained in their questions. Skimming was more sensible than close reading in this initial hunt for answers. Having key words as a focus for their search was especially important as the language was difficult for many of the children. Again the collaborative nature of the task was crucial: when the children found a section they

Interacting with the text, and monitoring understanding

thought might be useful they were encouraged to read it aloud and to work together to try to understand. The children were actively engaged in monitoring their own understanding rather than turning instantly to the teacher although, of course, this remained a final option.

Evaluating information

Several of the children discovered that different sources gave different information about, for example, how many people died and how many buildings were destroyed. This demonstrated the importance of both recording the source and questioning the credibility of the sources. They were encouraged to think for themselves why a newspaper account from the next day might say 20 houses were destroyed, whilst an insurance company account written a week later gave a different figure, and to decide which they thought was the more accurate figure.

Communicating information

The children then shared their questions and answers in a session on the carpet in order to build a complete picture of the event and to review their research. At this point, it might have been possible to produce a class flow chart or grid but time ran out. Finally, as planned, the children produced a finished version of their work for display.

Most of the class were paired so that more and less able readers worked together. One small group of four children with very low reading ability used a simple account of the events prepared by their teacher rather than the original documents. They interacted with this text by sequencing it. They did, however, join in the rest of the session with the other children.

In short, the teacher's awareness of ways of interacting with text enabled her to plan into her topic specific activities, such as question setting and adopting an appropriate reading strategy. She was not primarily concerned with the content of the sessions (although, of course, this had some importance) but rather with the processes which would help children become more effective users of information. A knowledge of theory had informed and illuminated her practice.

References

Anderson, R.C. (1977) 'The notion of schemata and the educational enterprise', in R.C. Anderson, R.J. Spiro, & W.E. Montague (eds), *Schooling and the acquisition of knowledge.* Hillsdale, N J: Lawrence Erlbaum

Anderson, R.C. & Pearson, P.D. (1984) 'A schema-theoretical view of basic processes in reading comprehension', in P.D. Pearson (ed.) *Handbook of reading research.* New York: Longman

Bransford, J. (1983) 'Schema activation – schema acquisition', in R.C. Anderson, J. Osborn & R.J. Tierney (eds), *Learning to read in American schools.* Hillsdale, N J: Lawrence Erlbaum

DES (1989) *Reading policy & practice at ages 5–14.* London: HMSO

O'Brien, J. (1994) 'Critical literacy in an early childhood classroom', *Australian Journal of Language and Literacy,* 17 (1): 36–44

Wilson, P.T. & Anderson, R.C. (1986) 'What they don't know will hurt them: the role of prior knowledge in comprehension', in J. Orasanu (ed), *Reading comprehension: from research into practice,* Hillsdale, N J: Lawrence Erlbaum

Lewis, M. & Wray, D. (1996) *Writing frames: scaffolding children's non-fiction writing in a range of genres.* Reading: Reading and Language Information Centre, University of Reading